# THE LITTLE BOOK OF
# ALGORITHMS

ISBN: 978-1-9161163-0-6

For the latest free download of this book, go to http://bit.do/LBOA

Email feedback and corrections to the author: william.lau@computingatschool.org.uk

Twitter: @MrLauLearning

*I dedicate this book to my colleagues and students at Central Foundation Boys' School. You have to be brave to choose (to teach or learn) computer science; it is not easy and it is not for the faint- hearted!*

*To Lloyd, Leila, Jaime, Gavin and the brave computer science students at CFBS - this is for you*

# CONTENTS

# PREFACE

This book is designed to help teachers and students build fluency in their Python programming. It is aimed at students who have already been introduced to the three basic programming constructs of structured programming, namely sequence, selection and iteration. The original aim was to help my Year 11 students with their GCSE Computer Science programming exam. However I hope many students and teachers will find this book useful. The algorithms are represented using Python as this is a popular language with a low threshold for learning.

I was inspired to write this book after reading articles by Scott Portnoff, Sue Sentance and Richard Pawson; three luminaries in the world of computer science education. All three have made me ask the question,

*"Why is learning programming so difficult?"*

Like many readers, I too found programming challenging and I am *still* learning! After teaching programming for the past seven years, I noticed that only a minority of my students felt confident enough to program independently after two years of instruction. Upon realising this, I knew I had to change my pedagogy.

I believe Scott Portnoff is correct; students do need to memorise some key programming constructs e.g. if statements, while loops and for loops. This will decrease cognitive load and enable students to practise more fluently. Portnoff's work was my starting point for this book. As a student of b-boy and hip-hop culture, I came across Joseph Schloss's book *Foundation* where he writes about a *musical* canon that exists for b-boys. To add to this theory, Jonathan Sacks argues that a *literary* canon is essential to a culture. In linking these three ideas together, I thought about creating a canon for programmers. Perhaps there is a set of programs which represent algorithms that every computer science student should familiarise themselves with?

I started to compile a list of programs based on my experience as a teacher and examiner. Many of the shorter programs are worth repeating until they are committed to memory and I admit that learning some of the longer programs by heart is both challenging and futile. Therefore, to help you develop fluency, I have also written some challenges based on this canon. These challenges should help you understand these programs by applying them.

Sue Sentance suggested in her introduction to programming courses, that we should introduce students to subroutines in their very first program. Richard Pawson goes one step further in edition 07 of the *Hello World* magazine; here Pawson puts forward a case for teaching using the functional programming (FP) paradigm from the outset. He makes a strong case for using functions which return values rather than containing inputs and outputs. This seems counterintuitive due to the perceived complexity of FP syntax, however there are three key arguments for using functions- unit testing of individual functions, code reusability and a separation of concerns. I would therefore encourage readers to write with functions from the very beginning. This seems daunting at first, however repetition will lead to fluency.

Despite the irrefutable advantages of FP, I have to be pragmatic and will include procedures (subroutines which do not return values) and also programs which do not use subroutines at all. Whilst, I recognise this might be a step away from the FP paradigm; students are likely to encounter simple structured algorithms up to at least GCSE level. Not including examples of both structured and FP paradigms would be doing our students a disservice. For some algorithms, the exclusion of functions also reduces complexity and cognitive load therefore providing a shallower learning curve.

In order to keep programs as short as possible and to improve readability, comments are not generally provided in the programs. Instead, a more detailed explanation is explained below each program. In lessons, I have found it useful to go through one or two algorithms at the front of the book with my students and then go to the associated challenge at the back. Alternatively, students may choose to work through the book independently in class or at home.

This book will hopefully help you to practise and develop fluency in your programming. Learning programming is similar to learning a musical instrument. Both involve practise and making lots of mistakes. Both also require perseverance to develop fluency. Keep going!

# LOWEST NUMBER

A program which takes two numbers as inputs and outputs the smallest number.

When you first started programming, you may have produced a program to ouput a lower number without using subroutines.

```
1    num1 = int(input("Enter the first number: "))
2    num2 = int(input("Enter the second number: "))
3
4    if num1 <= num2:
5        lowest = num1
6    else:
7        lowest = num2
8
9    print("The lowest number is " + str(lowest))
```

You may even be asked to write simple programs like this in your exams. However, good programmers write code which can be reused and tested in isolation (known as unit testing). Therefore, using a subroutine (also known as a subprogram) to create a procedure would produce a "better" program that is modular:

```
1    def lower_num(num1, num2):
2        if num1 <= num2:
3            lowest = num1
4        else:
5            lowest = num2
6
7        print("The lowest number is " + str(lowest))
8
9
10   first_num = int(input("Enter the first number: "))
11   second_num = int(input("Enter the second number: "))
12
13   lower_num(first_num, second_num)
```

Whilst the use of a procedure in the second program allows you to call the subprogram multiple times in the main program, it does not allow for full code re-use...

# LOWEST NUMBER CONTINUED...

...What happens if you wanted to use this lowest number later in the program? In this case, it makes sense to use a function. The key differentiator is that functions return values whereas procedures do not.

```
1   def lower_num(num1,num2):
2       if num1 <= num2:
3           return num1
4       else:
5           return num2
6
7
8   first_num = int(input("Enter the first number: "))
9   second_num = int(input("Enter the second number: "))
10
11  lowest = lower_num(first_num,second_num)
12
13  print("The lowest number is " + str(lowest))
```

- The function `lower_num` is defined on lines 1-5. We have to define functions before we can call (use) them.
- Usage of the function is demonstrated on lines 8-13. We still take two numbers as integer inputs on Lines 8-9.
- Line 11 calls the function `lower_num` with two arguments: the contents of `first_num` and `second_num` variables. These arguments are passed into the parameters `num1` and `num2` respectively[1]. The result is stored in the variable `lowest`.
- As the returned value is an integer, it is cast to a string on line 13 using str(lowest) so that it can be concatenated (the technical name for joining text) with the meaningful output message.

---

[1] Arguments and parameters should have different names even if they seem to serve the same purpose. In this case both num1 and first_num store the first number. However, the argument stored in the variable `first_num` has global scope, it can be accessed and changed anywhere in the program. The parameter `num1` has local scope, it is a local variable which can only be accessed in the subroutine.

# STRING CONCATENATION: MAKING A USERNAME

A subprogram which outputs a username based on a student's first name, surname and year of enrolment.

E.g. Connor Pearce 2019 should return 19CPearce.

```
1   def user_name(forename, last_name, year):
2      username_out = year[2:4] + forename[0] + last_name
3
4      print("Your user name is " + username_out)
5
6
7   first_name = input("Enter your first name: ")
8   surname = input("Enter your surname: ")
9   joined = input("Enter the year you joined the school: ")
10
11  user_name(first_name,surname,joined)
```

- The procedure `user_name` is defined on lines 1-4.
- Line 2: Strings can be sliced, with the first index being 0. In this case for the year, we start at 2 and stop at 4 (exclusive). This means we would slice year[2] and year[3] i.e. the last two digits of the `year`. These are concatenated with the first letter from the `forename` and the entire `last_name`.
- Lines 7-9: This shows how the procedure might be used. First the user's details are taken as string inputs .
- Then the procedure is called on line 11 with the user's details as arguments.
- The output is shown below:

```
Enter your first name: Connor
Enter your surname: Pearce
Enter the year you joined the school: 2019
Your username is 19CPearce
```

# STRING CONCATENATION: MAKING A USERNAME CONTINUED...

If you wanted to use this user_name procedure later to generate an email address, this would not be possible without duplication of code, it is therefore wise to rewrite this subprogram as a function. This is shown below:

```
1  def user_name(forename, last_name, year):
2      username_out = year[2:4] + forename[0] + last_name
3
4      return username_out
5
6
7  def main():
8      first_name = input("Enter your first name: ")
9      surname = input("Enter your surname: ")
10     year = input("Enter the year you joined the school: ")
11
12     gen_user_name = user_name(first_name, surname, year)
13     print("Your user name is " + gen_user_name)
14
15
16 if __name__ == '__main__':
17     main()
```

Here we introduce a programming convention of placing your main program in a main function. The main function should be the only function which contains inputs and ouputs in the entire program. From this main function you should call other functions, passing arguments into parameters. This process is known as parameter passing.

The main function above spans lines 7-13. Lines 16-17 ensure that your main function will be the first function to be run when the program is executed. __name__ == '__main__' by default. However, if the program is imported, the __name__ value becomes the module name, so you can selectively run or test functions. This is yet another advantage of using the functional programming paradigm.

# CALCULATE THE AREA OF A CIRCLE

A subprogram which calculates the area of a circle.

The example below is a function as it returns a value.

```
1   CONSTANT_PI=3.14159
2
3   def circle_area(radius_in):
4       area_out = CONSTANT_PI * radius_in**2
5       return area_out
6
7
8   radius = int(input("Enter the radius of the circle: "))
9   area = circle_area(radius)
10  print("The area of the circle is", area)
```

- Line 1: As the value of Pi *does not change whilst the program is running,* this is a constant. Programmers sometimes write constants in capitals and may give them meaningful names as shown.
- Line 3: The function `circle_area` is defined and has one parameter (a placeholder/variable) called `radius_in`.
- The `area_out` is calculated radius**2 may also be written as radius ^2 in other languages and psuedocode.
- Lines 8-10: This shows how the function may be used.
- Line 9: The `circle_area` is called and the `radius` is passed as an argument. The result is stored in the variable `area`.
- Line 10: In Python, we can also use a comma to concatenate the `area` to the output message. The advantage of using a comma to concatenate is that casting is done implicitly. This means the `str ()` function is not necessary. It is worth noting that concatenating with a comma will automatically add a space between concatenated strings.

# ODD OR EVEN?

A subprogram which checks if a number is odd or even. It will print a meaningful message accordingly. The program should loop until the user enters the sentinel value "STOP"

This is a procedure as no value is returned.

```
1   def is_odd(number_in):
2       if int(number_in) %2 == 0:
3           print("The number is even")
4       else:
5           print("The number is odd")
6
7
8   again = True
9   while again:
10    number = input("Enter a number")
11
12    if number != "STOP" :
13        odd = is_odd(number)
14    else:
15        again = False
```

- Line 2: The % symbol in Python means MODULO. So when we MOD2, we are checking for the remainder when dividing by 2
- Line 8: Sets a Boolean flag called `again` to True.
- Line 9: This is a Pythonic way of writing `while again == True:`
- Lines 11-12: Provided the user does not enter the sentinel value (also known as a rogue or trip value) of "STOP", the while loop will continue to call `is_odd` with each new number inputted to check if it is odd or even.
- This program could be improved by using function instead of a procedure. All inputs and outputs would take place outside of the function and you could also use a main function as shown previously on page 7.

# FOR LOOPS: OUTPUTTING NUMBERS

A subprogram which outputs all the numbers between a certain start and stop value (inclusive).

This is a procedure as it does not return a value.

```
1   def number_generator(start, stop):
2       for count in range(start,stop+1):
3           print(count)
4
5
6   start_num = int(input("Enter a start value"))
7   stop_num = int(input("Enter a stop value"))
8
9   number_generator(start_num, stop_num)
```

- The procedure `number_generator` is defined on lines 1-3.
- Line 2: uses a for loop to iterate from the start value to the stop value. In Python, the stop value is exclusive, so number_generator(1,10) would only print numbers 1 to 9, this is why we use `stop+1`.
- Lines 6-9 show how we would use the procedure.
- Lines 6-7: The user's details are taken as inputs .
- Then the procedure is called on line 9.

# WHILE LOOPS: NUMBER GUESSER

A program which generates a random number then asks the user to guess the random number. The program repeats until the correct number is guessed.

This is a function as the smallest number is returned.

```
1   import random
2   randomNumber = random.randint(1,10)
3   guess = 99
4   while guess != randomNumber:
5     guess = int(input("Guess the number between 1 and \
    10: "))
6     if guess == randomNumber:
7       print("Correct")
8     else:
9       print("Try again")
```

- Line 1: Imports the `random` module so that we can use the `randint` function to generate a random integer between 1 and 10 (inclusive).
- Unlike the previous program, we do not know how many times we need to repeat; the user could get the answer wrong 8 times or they could guess it first time. In these situations we use a conditional loop i.e. a while loop.
- Line 3: Sets an initial value that will never match the random number. This ensures the while loop runs at least once.
- Lines 8-9: If the user guess is incorrect, we return to the top of the loop i.e. line 5.

# LOWEST NUMBER IN A LIST

A program which iterates through a list of numbers and outputs the lowest number

```
1   numbers_list = [9,8,7,5,6,2,1,12,14,0,13]
2
3   lowest = numbers_list[0]
4
5   for count in range(len(numbers_list)):
6          if numbers_list[count] < lowest:
7               lowest = numbers_list[count]
8
9   print("The lowest number in the list is ", lowest)
```

- Line 3: We start with the hypothesis that the item at position 0 of numbers_list is the lowest.
- Line 5: We then iterate through the full length of the list, comparing each position with the initial value stored in lowest.
- Lines 6-7 If the current value is smaller than lowest, this number replaces the item in lowest.
- Line 9: When the for loop has finished and we have therefore reached the end of the list, we output the value of lowest.
- This can also be written as a function which takes a list as an argument.

```
1   def find_lowest(numbers_list_in):
2       lowest = numbers_list_in[0]
3
4       for count in range(len(numbers_list_in)):
5           if numbers_list_in[count] < lowest:
6              lowest = numbers_list_in[count]
7
8       return lowest
9
10  numbers_list = [9,8,7,5,6,2,1,12,14,0,13]
11  lowest_num = find_lowest(numbers_list)
12  print("The lowest number in the list is ", lowest_num)
```

# LINEAR SEARCH

Iterating through a list from start to finish as seen in the previous algorithm is effectively a linear search. We start at position 0 and continue checking each position from left to right until we reach the end. A meaningful message informs the user whether the item was found.

```
1   def linear_search(target):
2       names = ["Rocky", "Connor", "Jawwad",
3                 "Yacoub", "Cara", "Jess",
4                 "Jake", "Suki", "Zi", "Q"]
5
6       found = False
7
8       for count in range(len(names)):
9           if target == (names[count]):
10              print(target, "found at position", count)
11              found = True
12
13      if found == False:
14          print(target, "was not found")
15
16
17  name = input("Who are you looking for? ")
18  linear_search(name)
```

- For all searching algorithms, you should start by setting a Boolean flag to False. We do this on line 6.
- Lines 9-11: If the target matches the item in the array, the name is outputted and the Boolean flag is set to True.
- Lines 13-14: When we've iterated through the entire list, check to see if found is still False. If so, the item was not in the list.
- Line 18: Notice how we pass the argument stored in the variable called name into the parameter called target. The argument and parameter name are different so that we understand that their scope is different. The footnote on page 5 explains this in more detail.

13

# LINEAR SEARCH IN A 2D LIST

A program which searches for a student's results within a 2D list of exam scores.[1]

```
1   cs_scores=[["Jo","45","60","72"],["Zi","55","65","70"],
2   ["Ellie","71","78","78"],["Jessica","68","79","80"],
3   ["Abdul","65","70","71"]]
4
5   print("We will try to find the result for a given \
    student's exam")
6
7   name = input("Enter a student name: ")
8   exam_number = int(input("Enter the exam number: "))
9
10  found = False
11
12  for count in range(len(cs_scores)):
13      if name == cs_scores[count][0]:
14          found = True
15          result = cs_scores[count][exam_number]
16          print(name+ "'s result for exam", exam_number,\
    "was", result )
17
18  if found == False:
19      print(name, "cannot be found")
```

- Line 10: Use a variable to set a Boolean flag to False.
- Lines 12-14: if the name is located, the `found` flag is set to True and the result can be found by indexing the 2D list using the current `count` and the `exam_number`.
- Line 18: if we reach the end of the list and found is still False, then the number was not in the list.
- Lines 16 and 19: Output a meaningful message.

[1]Python does not have an array data structure. Instead it uses a list. The main differences between a list and an array is that lists allow the storage of mixed data types and they are dynamic (allow appending). I've tried to use single data types with the lists in this book so they appear more like arrays. I have also avoided the use of in-built list functions. This may seem strange and inefficient in places but it has been done as the GCSE exam will only feature arrays.

# BASIC LOGIN SYSTEM

A program which checks to see if the username and password matches the one in our program. The user gets three attempts.

```
1    username = "James"
2    password = "myPasswordIsDog!"
3    tries = 0
4
5    while tries < 3:
6        user_in = input("Enter the username")
7        pass_in = input("Enter the password")
8
9        if user_in == username:
10           if pass_in == password:
11               print("Logged in")
12               break
13           else:
14               print("Incorrect password")
15       else:
16           print("Incorrect username")
17
18       tries = tries+1
```

- Line 3: Initialises a while loop counter called `tries` to 0.
- Line 5: The while loop provides a maximum of 3 password attempts. We use a while loop because we do not know how many attempts the user will need to get the answer correct.
- Lines 10-12: If the correct `username` and `password` is supplied, we output a message and break out of the while loop. Otherwise, a meaningful error message is shown and the `tries` variable is incremented (Line 18).
- Line 18: This is also a common way to increase a score or counter.
- N.B. Storing the password as plaintext in the program that you are using is a really bad idea! Curious readers should visit: http://bit.do/hashing-python-passwords for more info.
-

# LOGIN SYSTEM BY READING A 2D LIST IN A FILE

A procedure which performs a linear search on a 2D list that is stored in a file.

| users.txt |
|---|
| [['lauw', 'insecurePwd'], ['vegaj', 'iLoveWebDesign'], ['lassamil', 'zeroDawn']]. |

```
1    def login():
2        username = input("What is your username")
3        password = input("What is your password")
4
5        newfile = open("users.txt","r")
6        users_2D = eval(newfile.read())
7        newfile.close()
8
9        found = False
10       for count in range(len(users_2D)):
11           if username == users_2D[count][0]:
12               found = True
13               if password == users_2D[count][1]:
14                   print("logged in")
15               else:
16                   print("incorrect password")
17                   login()
18
19       if found==False:
20           print("Invalid username")
21           login()
22
23   login()
```

- Line 5: Opens the file users.txt in read mode.
- Line 6: Reads the file. We have used the eval function which means that the translator will treat the text file's contents as a Python expression if the format is valid. In this case, it converts the contents of the text file into a 2D list and stores this under the identifier users_2D.
- Lines 17 and 21: calls the login procedure if the login fails i.e. it restarts the procedure.

# UNLIMITED PIN ATTEMPTS

A program which allows the user to enter a pin number. If the user gets the pin number wrong, the program keeps asking them to enter a correct pin.

N.B. An unlimited number of attempts is a bad idea as it allows for brute force hacking. However, this is a common algorithm that is used in guessing games e.g. guess the number.

```
1  pin = ""
2  while pin != "1984":
3     pin = input("Please enter the pin")
4
5     if pin == "1984":
6        print("Logged in")
7     else:
8        print("Incorrect pin")
```

- The program keeps looping while the pin is not equal to 1984. It is very similar to the program on page 11.
- Line 1: Sets an initial value that is not equal to the pin. This ensures the while loop runs at least once.
- Line 3 asks the user to enter their pin.
- Lines 5-8 check to see if the pin matches, a meaningful message is produced depending on the outcome.

# TOTAL OF A LIST

A program which adds up numbers in a list

```
1   number_list = [9, 8, 3, 5, 4, 1, 8, 4, 1]
2
3   total = 0
4
5   for count in range(len(number_list)):
6       total = total + number_list[count]
7
8   print("The total sum of the list is ", total)
```

- Line 3: Defines the variable `total` and initialises it to 0.
- Line 5: Iterates through the length of the list, 0 to 9 (exclusive).
- Line 6: Takes the current value of total and adds the current value in the list to the total. This cumulative total is commonly used for scores and timers in programs.
- A functional programming approach is also shown below:

```
1   def total_list (number_list_in):
2       total = 0
3
4       for count in range(len(number_list)):
5           total = total + number_list[count]
6
7       return total #the total is returned
8
9
10  def main():
11      # The main function contains all inputs and outputs
12      number_list = [9, 8, 3, 5, 4, 1, 8, 4, 1]
13
14      op = input("Do you wish to find the mean, lowest \
        value, highest value or the total of the list?")
15
16      # Call the relevant function based on the user input
17      if op == "total":
18          total_out = total_list(number_list)
19          print("The total sum of the list is ", total_out)
20      # Elifs would go here
21
22  # Call the main function
23  main()
```

# TOTAL OF A 2D LIST

A program which adds up each student's scores in a 2D list i.e. a row or sub list

```
1   cs_scores = [["Karman","45","60","72"],
2                ["Daniel","55","65","70"],
3                ["Giacomo","71","78","78"],
4                ["Jessica","68","79","80"],
5                ["Edie","98","85","91"]]
6
7   total = 0
8   for student in range(len(cs_scores)):
9       for exam in range(1,4):
10          total = total + int(cs_scores[student][exam])
11      print("Total for",cs_scores[student][0],"=",total)
12      total = 0
```

- In the program above we are trying to calculate each student's total, so the student is in the first loop. This is also known as the outer loop.
- Line 8: Iterate through 0 to 5 (exclusive) i.e each student .
- Line 9: Now starting with student 0 i.e. Karman, enter the nested inner loop through exams 1 to 4 (exclusive) i.e. exams 1-3.
- Line 10: Add the score to the running total.
- Line 11: Output the student's total.
- Line 12: Reset the total  variable to 0 so that we can now start the second iteration of the student loop and calculate the total of Daniel's exams.

# CONVERTING BINARY TO DENARY

A subprogram which takes a 4-bit binary string as an argument and returns the denary equivalent

```
1   def binary_to_denary(binary):
2       bit1 = int(binary[3])*1
3       bit2 = int(binary[2])*2
4       bit3 = int(binary[1])*4
5       bit4 = int(binary[0])*8
6
7       denary_out = bit1 + bit2 + bit3 + bit4
8       return denary_out
9
10
11  def main():
12      binary_in = input("Enter the binary string")
13      denary = binary_to_denary(binary_in)
14      print("The binary value", binary_in, "in denary \
        is", denary)
15
16
17  if __name__ == '__main__':
18      main()
```

- Lines 17-18: The default value for __name__ in every Python program is '__main__' and so the main function is called.
- Line 12: Asks the user for a binary string.
- Line 13: Calls the binary_to_denary function, passing the binary string as an argument. The returned value will be stored in the denary variable and output on Line 14.
- Line 1: Defines a function called binary_to_denary and takes the binary_in string as an argument.
- Lines 2-5: Slices each individual digit and multiplies it by its relevant place value.
- Lines 7-8: The total is calculated and returned.
- Line 14: The denary equivalent is outputted with a meaningful message.

# CONVERTING DENARY TO BINARY

A program which converts a denary value between 0-15 to a 4-bit binary value

```
1   denary = int(input("Enter the denary number between \
    0 and 15"))
2
3   binary = ["0","0","0","0"]
4
5   if denary > 15:
6       print("error")
7   if denary >=8 and denary <=15:
8       binary[0] = "1"
9       denary = denary - 8
10  if denary >=4:
11      binary[1] = "1"
12      denary = denary - 4
13  if denary >=2:
14      binary[2] = "1"
15      denary = denary - 2
16  if denary >=1:
17      binary[3] = "1"
18
19  for count in range(len(binary)):
20      print(binary[count],end="")
```

- Line 3: With binary numbers, we cannot use the integer data type. A default string of "0000" also cannot be used as strings in Python are not mutable. Having four bits like the previous program could work, but I would have to define and initialise each bit. This could create up to four lines of extra code. I therefore decided to use a list as lists are mutable.
- Lines 7-17: This models the "left-to-right" process of checking how many 8s, 4s, 2s and 1s go into a number between 0-15.
- Lines 19-20: This is a way to iterate through the list and print each element without commas, brackets and new lines. The end="" means at the end of each print, do not add anything, as a default end="\n" i.e. a new line at the end of every print.

# CHALLENGES

You've written a few programs in class and at home. Now is the time to practise. The challenges will start by getting you to modify existing programs in this book and progressively get more difficult.

Try to write your answer without looking back at the programs at the front of this book. If you really need a hint, page numbers are provided. You can check your answers against the solutions

Pro tip: Always answer in pencil first, you can go over these in pen afterwards.

# CHALLENGE 1: HIGHEST NUMBER

Write a subprogram that has three parameters, num1, num2 and num3. The program should take three numbers as arguments and return the highest number.

Hint: You may consult the lowest number program on page 5.

```
def highest_number (num1, num2, num3):
        if num1 >= num2 and num1 >= num3:
```

# CHALLENGE 2: UNIQUE USERNAME

Write a subprogram which generates a username for a teacher based on their first name and surname. The format should be their surname, followed by the first letter of their first name. The program should check to see if the username already exists in users.txt and if so, a unique username should be generated by appending a "#" symbol. E.g. if a teacher joins the school called Winnie Lau, their username would be LauW# .

Hint: You may consult programs on page 6 and 16

| users.txt |
|---|
| [['LauW', 'insecurePwd'], ['VegaJ', 'iLoveWebDesign'], ['LassamiL', 'zeroDawn']] |

```
def generate_username(firstname, lastname):
    username = _____


    #check to see if the username already exists
    users_file = open(_____, _____)
    usernames = eval(_____)
    users_file.close()


    for count in range(len(_____)):
        if _____ ==username:
            username = _____
    return _____
```

# CHALLENGE 2 CONTINUED...

Write a program which asks for a teacher's first name and surname. Then demonstrate how you would call the function on the previous page to generate a username and output this in a meaningful message.

The next two pages are provided so that you can practise Challenges 1 and 2 without the writing frames. It's important that you keep challenging yourself and eventually you should be able to write these programs independently.

# CHALLENGE 1: HIGHEST NUMBER

Write a subprogram that has three parameters, num1, num2 and num3. The program should take three numbers as arguments and return the highest number.

# CHALLENGE 2: UNIQUE USERNAME

Write a subprogram which generates a username for a teacher based on their first name and surname. The format should be their surname, followed by the first letter of their first name. The program should check to see if the username already exists in users.txt and if so, a unique username should be generated by appending a "#" symbol. E.g. if a teacher joins the school called Winnie Lau, their username would be LauW# .

| users.txt |
|---|
| [['LauW', 'insecurePwd'], ['VegaJ', 'iLoveWebDesign'], ['LassamiL', 'zeroDawn']] |

# CHALLENGE 3: VOLUME OF A CUBOID

Write a subprogram that takes the length, width and height as arguments and return the volume of the cuboid.

After writing the function, show how you might use the function to output an answer with a meaningful message.

Hint: You may consult the "area of a circle" program on page 8.

# CHALLENGE 4: ROLL A DOUBLE TO START

Write a program which simulates two dice being rolled. Output the values of both dice. Keep prompting the user to roll the dice until the two dice match e.g. Double 6. When the user roles a double, output the message "Game loading". For all other combinations, ask the user to press Enter to roll again.

Hint: You may consult the while loop programs on pages 11 and 17.

# CHALLENGE 5: COUNTING VOWELS

Iterate through the sentence below and count how many times each vowel occurs. At the end of the program, ouput the number of As, Es, Is, Os and Us with a meaningful message.

sentence = "Learning programming is similar to learning a musical instrument. Both involve practise and making lots of mistakes. Both also require perseverance to develop fluency. Keep going!"

Hint: See programs on pages 10, 12, 15. You can iterate through the sentence in the same way you iterate through a list or list.

```
def vowel_counter(sentence):
    A = 0
    E = 0
    I = 0


    for count in range(
        if sentence[count].upper() == "A":
```

# CHALLENGE 5: COUNTING VOWELS

Iterate through the sentence below and count how many times each vowel occurs. At the end of the program, ouput the number of As, Es, Is, Os and Us with a meaningful message.

sentence = "Learning programming is similar to learning a musical instrument. Both involve practise and making lots of mistakes. Both also require perseverance to develop fluency. Keep going!"

Extra challenge: Store the vowel counters in a list or 2D list.

# CHALLENGE 5 CONTINUED...

# CHALLENGE 6: HIGHEST NUMBER IN A LIST

Write a program which iterates through a list of numbers and outputs the highest number

I dare you to pass the list into a function!
Hint: Page 12

numbers = [9, 8, 72, 22, 21, 81, 2, 1, 11, 76, 32, 54]

# CHALLENGE 7: WEAK PASSWORD?

Write a program which asks the user to enter a desired password. Perform a linear search through a list of obvious (weak) passwords. If the user's password is found in the obvious passwords list, output a message to tell them it is weak and would be easily hacked using a brute force attack.

Extra challenge: You may also want to add in various validation checks. One example might be a length check, so if the password does not meet a particular length it is also declared weak. Meaningful messages are necessary for each different validation check.

obvious = ["password", "qwerty", "hello123", "letmein", "123456"]

# CHALLENGE 8: GRADE BOUNDARIES

An A-Level student wants to find out how many marks are required to receive a certain grade. Write a subprogram that takes a user's desired grade as an argument and then iterates through the 2D list to return the number of marks they need for that grade.

Hint: Page 14

```
def marks(_____):
    grades = [ ["A*", "90"], ["A", "83"], ["B", "72"], ["C", "60"], ["D", "49"], ["E", "30"] ]
```

# CHALLENGE 9: PENALTY SHOOTOUT

Write a program which simulates a penalty shootout. The computer is the goalkeeper and dives a random direction or stays in the centre each turn. The keeper's move is generated but not outputted at first. The user takes a penalty by typing in "left", "right" or "centre". The keeper's move is then outputted. If the player typed left and the keeper dives left, the penalty is saved etc. The program repeats 5 times. After 5 penalties, the winner is announced with a meaningful message.

Hint: Pages 10 and 11. I strongly advise using a pencil for this one!

```
import random


keeper = ["left", "centre", "right"]
```

# More space on next page...

# CHALLENGE 9: PENALTY SHOOTOUT CONTINUED...

# CHALLENGE 10: REGISTER AN ACCOUNT

Write a subprogram to allow a teacher to register a new account. The subprogram should take the username and password as arguments and write these details to the existing users.txt file shown opposite. We can assume this subprogram used the `generate_username` function on page 24 to for the username and a password is inputted separately in the main function.

Hint: Use the comments on the opposite page as skeleton code to structure your subprogram

```
def new_user(username_in, password_in):
```

# CHALLENGE 10: REGISTER AN ACCOUNT CONTINUED...

| users.txt |
|---|
| [['lauw', 'insecurePwd'], ['vegaj', 'iLoveWebDesign'], ['lassamil', 'zeroDawn']] |

# define a function called new_user with two parameters: username and password

#open the file in read mode

#use eval to read in the 2D list

#close the file

#make a new list for the new user

#append the username to the new user list

#append the password to the same list

#append this new user list to the existing 2D list that we read in

#open the file in write mode

#cast the updated 2D list as a string and write this string to the file

#close the file

# CHALLENGE 11: AVERAGE OF A LIST

Write a subprogram called mean_of_list that takes a list of numbers as an argument and returns the mean average.

Write the main function which contains your list and which calls the subprogram (function)

Hint: Pages 7, 18, 20

```
def mean_of_list(numbers_list_in):
```

# CHALLENGE 12: TOTAL FOR EACH EXAM IN A 2D LIST

Recall the program which adds up each student's scores in a 2D list i.e. a row or sub list on page 19. Write a program which will output the total for each exam with a meaningful message.

Hint: As the focus is on each *exam* rather than each student, the outer for loop will be for each *exam.* Remember to reset the total after each iteration of the inner loop.

```
cs_scores = [["Karman","45","60","72"],
["Daniel","55","65","70"],
["Giacomo","71","78","78"],
["Jessica","68","79","80"],
["Edie","98","85","91"]]


total = 0


for exam in range(_____):
```

# CHALLENGE 13: AVERAGE FOR EACH STUDENT IN A 2D LIST

Write a subprogram that takes the 2D list of exam results as an argument and outputs the mean average for each student.

Hint: Remember to reset the total to 0 after outputting the average for each student

```
cs_scores = [["Karman","45","60","72"],
["Daniel","55","65","70"],
["Giacomo","71","78","78"],
["Jessica","68","79","80"],
["Edie","98","85","91"]]


def mean_student(                    ):
```

# CHALLENGE 14: CONVERTING HEXADECIMAL TO DENARY

Write a function which takes in 1 hexadecimal digit as an argument and returns the denary equivalent.

Write a main function which asks the user to input a hexadecimal value and then passes this value to the function you have written.

Hint: Pages 7 and 20

# CHALLENGE 15: CALCULATING THE FILE SIZE OF A SOUND FILE

The size of a sound file can be calculated by using the following formula:

File size = sampling frequency * bit depth * channels * duration

The answer will be given in bits, therefore we can convert this to kilobytes by dividing the answer by (8 * 1024.)

Write a subprogram which takes the sampling frequency, bit depth, channels and duration of a sound file and returns the file size. This can then be outputted in Kilobytes and Megabytes.

# CHALLENGE 15: CALCULATING THE FILE SIZE OF A SOUND FILE CONTINUED...

Use the space below to finish the function and to show how it may be called.

# SPACE FOR FURTHER PRACTISE AND NOTES

# SOLUTIONS

Eirini Kolaiti came up with the great idea of putting example solutions to the challenges at the back of the book. I will also post these solutions online at: http://bit.do/LBOA

There is always more than one way to solve a problem. Even if the algorithm is well-defined, there may be alternative programming approaches. The following pages present examples which you can compare to your own answers. Comments have been provided to aid your understanding, you should develop the habit of commenting all your programs.

Do not worry if you have written an alternative solution. Also be aware that these solutions were not produced by typing the whole program out and running them with no syntax and logic errors on the first time! There was a debugging process as I wrote each line or block of code. Encountering errors whilst iteratively testing is the "normal" way to develop programs.

## CHALLENGE 1:

```python
#define a function called highest_num with three parameters
def highest_number (num1, num2, num3):
    # return the highest number
    if num1 >= num2 and num1 >= num3:
        return num1
    elif num2 >= num1 and num2 >= num3:
        return num2
    else:
        return num3


first = int(input("Enter the first number: "))
second = int(input("Enter the second number: "))
third = int(input("Enter the third number: "))

#   call the highest_number function and pass the contents of
#   first, second and third variables as arguments into the
#   parameters num1, num2, num3
highest = highest_number(first,second,third)

#output the highest number with a meaningful message
print("The highest number is " + str(highest))
```

## CHALLENGE 2:

```
def generate_username (firstname, lastname):
    #  create username based on the lastname and first intiial
    username = lastname + firstname[0]

    #  open the file in read mode and evaluate its contents
    users_file = open("users.txt","r")
    usernames = eval(users_file.read())
    users_file.close()

    #  check the entire 2D array to see if the username exists
    for count in range(len(usernames)):
        #  if the username exists, add a # symbol
        if usernames[count][0] == username:
            username = username + "#"

    #  return the final username
    return username


forename = input("Enter your first name: ")
surname = input("Enter your surname: ")

username_out = generate_username(forename, surname)
print("Your username is " + str(username_out))
```

## CHALLENGE 3:

```
def cuboid_volume (length, width, height):
    volume = length * width * height

    return volume


length_in = int(input("Enter the length of the cuboid: "))
width_in = int(input("Enter the width of the cuboid: "))
height_in = int(input("Enter the height of the cuboid: "))

volume_out = cuboid_volume(length_in, width_in, height_in)
print("The volume of the cuboid is " + str(volume_out))
```

# CHALLENGE 4:

```python
import random

#  initialise the dice with two different values so the
#  program runs at least once
dice1 = 1
dice2 = 2

while dice1 != dice2:
   dice1 = random.randint(1,6)
   dice2 = random.randint(1,6)

   print("Dice 1 rolled:" + str(dice1))
   print("Dice 2 rolled:" + str(dice2))

   if dice1 == dice2:
     print("Game loading")
   else:
     # Use input to enable the user to press enter to continue
     #  looping
     again = input("Press enter to roll again")
```

# CHALLENGE 5:

```
def vowel_counter(sentence):
    A = 0
    E = 0
    I = 0
    O = 0
    U = 0

    for count in range(len(sentence)):
        #  The .upper() casts the current letter to an upper
case
        #  Without .uppper(), we would write
        #  if sentence[count] == "A" or sentence[count] ==
"a":
        if sentence[count].upper() == "A":
            A = A+1
        elif sentence[count].upper() == "E":
            E = E+1
        elif sentence[count].upper() == "I":
            I = I+1
        elif sentence[count].upper() == "O":
            O =O+1
        elif sentence [count].upper() == "U":
            U = U+1

    #  using comma to concatenate in Python means we can cast
    #  the integer values implicitly without using str()
    print("The number of A's:", A)
    print("The number of E's:", E)
    print("The number of I's:", I)
    print("The number of O's:", O)
    print("The number of U's:", U)


sentence = "Learning programming is similar to learning a
musical instrument. Both involve practise and making lots of
mistakes. Both also require perseverence to develop fluency.
Keep going!"

vowel_counter(sentence)
```

## CHALLENGE 6:

```
numbers = [9, 8, 72, 22, 21, 81, 2, 1, 11, 76, 32, 54]

highest = numbers[0]

for count in range(len(numbers)):
   if highest < numbers[count]:
      highest = numbers[count]

print("The highest number is", highest)


#  An alternative approach using a function:

numbers = [9, 8, 72, 22, 21, 81, 2, 1, 11, 76, 32, 54]

def highest_num(numbers_in):
   highest = numbers[0]

   for count in range(len(numbers)):
      if highest < numbers[count]:
         highest = numbers[count]

   return highest

highest_out = highest_num(numbers)
print("The highest number is", highest_out)
```

## CHALLENGE 7:

```
obvious = ["password", "qwerty", "hello123", "letmein",
"123456"]

password = input("Please enter a password: ")

#  A basic linear search which iterates through the obvious
#  list to check for matches against the password
for count in range(len(obvious)):
   if password == obvious[count]:
      print("This password is weak. It uses a common word or \
phrase making it susceptible to a brute force attack")

#  Length check
if len(password) < 8:
   print("Your password is too short. Please use at least \
8 characters")
```

## CHALLENGE 7 CONTINUED...

```
#   initialise some counter variables for different types of
#   characters
char = 0
num = 0
upper = 0
lower = 0

for count in range(len(password)):
   #  A linear search to check if the character is a digit
   if password[count].isdigit():
      num = num+1
   #  A check to see if the character is an upper or lower char
   elif password[count].isalpha():
      char = char+1
      if password[count].isupper():
         upper = upper+1
      elif password[count].islower():
         lower = lower+1

if num == 0:
   print("To make your password more secure, you could include \
numbers")
if upper == 0 or lower ==0:
   print("To make your password more secure, you could include \
upper and lower case letters")
if char == 0:
   print("To make your password more secure, you could include \
letters")
if num  > 0 and char > 0 and upper > 0 and lower > 0:
   print("Your password meets the minimum length requirements \
and contains a mixture of numbers, characters, upper and lower
case letters.")
```

## CHALLENGE 8:

```
def marks(grade_in):
   grades = [["A*","90"],["A","83"],["B","72"],["C","60"],
["D","49"],["E","30"]]

   for count in range(len(grades)):
      if grades[count][0] == grade_in:
         return grades[count][1]


grade = input("What grade do you wish to achieve")
mark_req = marks(grade)
print("For grade", grade, "you need to gain", mark_req)
```

## CHALLENGE 9:

```
import random

keeper = ["left", "centre", "right"]

keeper_score = 0
player_score = 0

for count in range(5):
   dive = random.choice(keeper)

   player = input("Do you wish to shoot to the left, centre or
right: ")

   print("Keeper went to the", dive)

   if keeper == player:
      print("Penalty saved")
      keeper_score = keeper_score+1
   else:
      print("GOAAAAAAL!")
      player_score = player_score+1


if keeper_score > player_score:
    print("Keeper wins", keeper_score, "-", player_score)
else:
    print("You win!", player_score, "-", keeper_score)
```

## CHALLENGE 10:

```
def new_user(username_in, password_in):
   users_file = open("users.txt", "r")
   users = eval(users_file.read())
   users_file.close()

   new_user = []
   new_user.append(username_in)
   new_user.append(password_in)

   users.append(new_user)

   users_file = open("users.txt", "w")
   users_file.write(str(users))
   users_file.close()
```

## CHALLENGE 11:

```
def mean_of_list(numbers_list_in):
    total = 0
    for count in range(len(numbers_list_in)):
        total = total + numbers_list_in[count]

    # divide by the length of the list to find the mean
    average = total / len(numbers_list_in)
    return average


def main():
    numbers_list = [0,7,5,3,22,23,11,34,51,32,5,3,1]

    mean = mean_of_list(numbers_list)
    print("The mean average of", numbers_list, "=", mean)


main()

# A better way to call main in case the file is imported:
# if __name__ == '__main__':
#     main()
```

## CHALLENGE 12:

```
cs_scores=[["Karman","45","60","72"],
           ["Daniel","55","65","70"],
           ["Giacomo","71","78","78"],
           ["Jessica","68","79","80"],
           ["Edie","98","85","91"]]

total = 0

for exam in range(1,4):
# iterate through each exam
    for student in range(len(cs_scores)):
    # update the total by iterating through each student
        total = total + int(cs_scores[student][exam])

    # calculate the total
    print("Total for exam num", exam, "=", total)
    # reset the total before starting on the next exam
    total = 0
```

## CHALLENGE 13:

```python
cs_scores=[["Karman","45","60","72"],["Daniel","55","65","70"],
           ["Giacomo","71","78","78"],["Jessica","68","79","80"],
           ["Edie","98","85","91"]]


def mean_student(scores_in):
    total = 0

    for exam in range(1,4):
    #   iterate through each exam
        for student in range(len(cs_scores)):
        #   update the total by iterating through each student
            total = total + int(cs_scores[student][exam])

        #   calculate and output the mean
        mean = total / len(cs_scores)
        print("Mean average for exam num", exam, "=", mean)

        #   reset the total before starting on the next exam
        total = 0


mean_student(cs_scores)
```

## CHALLENGE 14:

```python
def hex_to_denary(hex_in):
    #   only convert values A to F
    hex_A_to_F = [["A","10"],["B","11"],["C","12"],["D","13"],
["E","14"],["F","15"]]

    convert = False
    for count in range(len(hex_A_to_F)):
        if hex_in == hex_A_to_F[count][0]:
            convert = True
            return int(hex_A_to_F[count][1])

    #   if values are not A to F i.e. 1 to 9, return these as
    #   integers
    if convert == False:
        return int(hex_in)

def main():

    hexi = input("Enter a hex digit to convert: ")
    hex_out = hex_to_denary(hexi)
    print("The denary equivalent is", hex_out)
```

## CHALLENGE 15:

```
def file_size(frequency, bits, channels, duration):
    size = frequency * bits * channels * duration
    return size


def main():

    freq = int(input("Enter the frequency in Hz: "))
    bit_depth = int(input("Enter the bit depth: "))
    channel = int(input("Enter the number of channels: "))
    length = int(input("Enter the duration of the sound file in \
seconds: "))

    size_out = file_size(freq, bit_depth, channel, length)
    size_kb = size_out / (8 * 1024)
    size_mb = size_kb / 1024
    print("The file size is", size_kb, "KB")
    print("The file size is", size_mb, "MB")


main()

#  A better way to call main in case the file is imported:
#  if __name__ == '__main__':
#      main()
```

# FURTHER READING

## FOR STUDENTS AND TEACHERS:

| | |
|---|---|
| Coding Club Python Basics Level 1 (2012) [1]<br>Coding Club Next Steps Level 2 (2013) | Chris Roffey |
| Making Games with Python and Pygame (2012)<br>Automate The Boring Stuff With Python (2015)<br>www.inventwithpython.com | Al Sweigart |
| www.pythonprogramming.net<br>See also: Youtube channel- sentdex | Sentdex |
| www.kidscancode.org<br>See also: Youtube channel- KidsCanCode | Chris and Priya<br>Bradfield |
| Youtube channel– MrLauLearning | William Lau |
| Youtube channel– Tech With Tim | Tech With Tim |
| Youtube channel- Corey Schafer | Corey Schafer |
| Youtube channel– Computerphile | Computerphile |
| How We Learn (2014) | Benedict Carey |
| Why We Sleep (2017) | Matthew Walker |

## FOR TEACHERS:

| | |
|---|---|
| Teaching Computing in Secondary Schools | William Lau |
| Computer Science Education | Edited by Sue Sentance,<br>Erik Barendsen and<br>Carsten Schulte |
| Teach Like a Champion 2.0 | Doug Lemov |
| Tools for Teaching | Fred Jones |

[1]Two brilliant books for absolute beginners. These "how-to" guides take you step by step through the basic programming structures required to access most of the material in this book.

# ACKNOWLEDGEMENTS

My knowledge and understanding of programming was initially developed by attending courses run by Ilia Avroutine, Darren Travi, Graham Bradshaw, David Batty and Sarah Shakibi. I have also benefitted greatly from the mentoring of Merijn Broeren, Elizabeth Hidson and Andy Swann.

The generosity of those who produce resources to teach programming such as Chris Roffey, Al Sweigart and Sentdex along with the wider CAS and Facebook community is also a great source of inspiration. To all of the aforementioned, I am indebted. You have given me the confidence to keep developing my programming skills independently and to eventually share these skills with you on CAS, Facebook, Youtube and in my books.

To further my understanding of programming, I have had the great privilege of sharing thoughts with Peter Kemp, Alex Parry, Eirini Kolaiti, Richard Pawson, Scott Portnoff, Sue Sentance and Meg Ray. All of these brilliant teachers and programmers read early drafts of this book and their comments have improved the book significantly.

I hope that my compromise of including procedures as well as non-modular programs is forgiven. I have to be realistic and acknowledge that for all novices, writing programs without subroutines is a starting point and an achievement in itself. There are many solutions to a given algorithm and provided that the output is correct and the algorithm is reasonably efficient, we should recognise these as correct (up to GCSE level) even if subroutines are not used.

I thank my colleagues, particularly Lloyd Stevens, Leila Lassami, Jaime Vega, Gavin Tong, Edward Swire, Pat Cronin and Jamie Brownhill at Central Foundation Boys' School (CFBS). They have supported me with their time, patience and agreeable responses to my (occasionally unreasonable) demands! I also thank the students at CFBS whose hard work have provided me with further motivation to improve my teaching . Our students always inspire us to be better .

To Suki, Zi and Q, this book would not be possible without you. Many people ask me how I have time to write these books and my answer is, "I have an understanding family!" Thank you for your continued support.

28540646R00041

Printed in Great Britain
by Amazon